A First Drawing Comics Book

C000100285

ORANGUTAN Can't DRAW COMICS

Noodle Juice Ltd

www.noodle-juice.com

Stonesfield House, Stanwell Lane, Great Bourton, Oxfordshire, OX17 1QS

First published in Great Britain 2023

Copyright © Noodle Juice Ltd 2023

Text by Luke Newell and Noodle Juice 2023

Illustrations by Luke Newell and Mr Griff 2023

All rights reserved

Printed in China

A CIP catalogue record of this book is available from the British Library.

ISBN: 978-1-915613-21-9

1 3 5 7 9 10 8 6 4 2

This book is made from FSC®-certified paper. By choosing this book, you help to take care of the world's forests. Learn more: www.fsc.org.

I like comics cos they taste like chicken!

Orangutan can't draw comics, but YOU can!

Contents

Darling, you'll learn about story, characters, text and even how to make a dummy book.

I'm going to need all your help!

Welcome to Orangutan Can't Draw Comics!

Ever since Rhino learned how to draw, he's been insufferable! Always showing off to the gang and pointing out that he's so much better than the rest of them. Rhino says, 'Orangutan might be great at drawing landscapes, but he's useless at comics – and that's what everyone wants to read these days!'

So Orangutan has decided that it's time he learned how to draw comics, and you're welcome to join him along the way.

Meet the team

Tiger

Artist in residence.

Orangutan

Wants to create his own comic and show Rhino just how good an artist he really is.

> I can draw and paint, but I have no idea where to start when it comes to comics. Surely it can't be that hard?

> Comics – aren't they funny people who stand on stage and have tomatoes thrown at them? I like tomatoes.

Rhinoceros

Is still showing off!

Crocodile

Tends to make a mess, and was brought up in a sewer.

What you will need

Plain A4 or A3 paper sheets

It's a good idea to work on loose paper as it's useful to be able to ROTATE the page (see page 27), or stick bits together if you need to. Many comic book artists prefer to work on large sheets of paper and then shrink their pictures down.

Blue and black pencils

Colour pencils are GREAT as they're usually quite soft. Use a lighter colour for when you're working things out. Then when you're happy, go over the top with a darker colour.

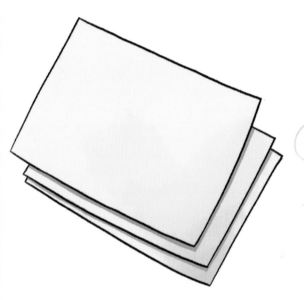

Erasers

While it can be helpful to leave any mistakes you make when drawing pictures, when drawing comics, it's better to keep your lines clean.

Sticky notes

These are great for when you are story-boarding (see page 6). You can move the action around really easily until you have the right flow.

A ruler

Rulers are super helpful because you'll often need to draw out your comic grids. In this instance straight lines really help to organise the eye.

Final artwork

This is completely up to you – are you drawing in pen and ink, felt-tip pen, pencil or digitally on a computer or tablet?

What Is a Comic?

Comics are, quite simply...

SEPARATE PICTURES IN SEQUENCE THAT TELL A STORY.

Sometimes with text, sometimes only with pictures. Comics can be printed, available online in a digital format, or even drawn on a wall!

Sequential pictures are incredibly powerful. Apart from speech, it's the earliest form of storytelling.

OH, THE HORROR!

But far from being old-fashioned, we live in a time where there has never been SO MUCH visual storytelling. Movies, TV shows, video games, websites and social media all have their content planned out in some part with a storyboard...

Which is basically a comic made for the screen. Learn to make a comic and you're halfway to making a movie!

Comics, tragics, magics, historics, poetics...

Many people think of fantasy, action or humour when they think of comics, but as we've said, a comic is just a way of telling a story. In the same way that you can write a sentence, or talk about ANYTHING you like, the same goes for comics. It is writing, with pictures.

Ink and brush?

Also, your pictures don't have to look a certain way because they're in a comic. You might assume they need to look like superheroes or cartoons, but they could be stick men, or drawn in pencil. You could create collages or paint in watercolour. You could even use photographs.

However, making a comic can be a LOT of work, so you may want to keep things simple at first! Use whichever style you feel most comfortable with AND tells the story most clearly.

Keep things simple, you say? Not while doing a handstand, then...

How do people find comics?

Traditionally comics would be mass printed on paper and then sold through bookshops, specialist comic stores or even newsagents and grocers. They still are, and certain kinds of comics, such as Japanese manga, have become extremely popular in recent years. But it's never been easier to get your comics out into the world. You can make them available online in a digital format, or you could print from your computer to make copies to give to friends or even sell! (See page 94 for tips.)

I leave my comics under rocks for people to find!

Comics are made all over the world, and are read differently according to where they are made. For example, to read manga, you read top to bottom, BUT FROM RIGHT TO LEFT.

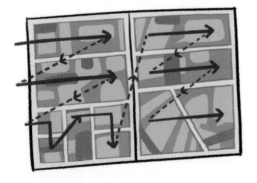

In this book, we're assuming you're reading these words from left to right (if you're not, this won't be making ANY sense,) so we'll be making our comics read from left to right, top to bottom. But in yours, it's up to you!

Could you make a circular comic that you can read forever?

GENERALLY, people have come to expect images to flow in the same direction that the text does (in their particular culture) ... but this doesn't mean you shouldn't PLAY with the format, do something surprising! It's your comic creation, after all.

TOP TIP #1 Comic Words

When drawing comics, there are plenty of new words to learn. Here's a handy set of definitions that will help you understand your gutters from your bubbles!

Letters drawn in outline, that leave space to be coloured in, are called OPEN LETTERS.

Outlines with jagged edges that surround the title are called SPLASH BALLOONS.

The first page of a story, with a large illustration, is called a SPLASH PAGE.

A single illustration on a page is called a PANEL. Pages can be made up of any number of panels.

The space in between the panels is called a GUTTER.

Words that share what a character is thinking are surrounded by THOUGHT BALLOONS.

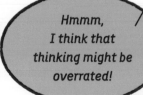

The small circles are called BUBBLES.

Speech is contained within DIALOGUE BALLONS. If words are emphasised, they are known as BOLD LETTERING.

The links on a dialogue balloon that show who is speaking are called POINTERS.

*DIALOGUE BALLOONS, eh? I think they look more like **DIALOGUE MELONS!** Yummy!*

If the balloon has a dotted line, the character is whispering.

Words that are talking directly to the reader – such as setting the scene, or pointing something out – are called CAPTIONS.

BILL IS BECOMING IRRITATED...

IT LOOKS AS IF FRED IS GOING TO GET HIS COMEUPPANCE!

FSSSSS
TNT
TNT

FFFBOOOMSH!!

Sound effects are often illustrated using large and bold lettering.

I can make some sound effects of my own. Normally after a tin of beans, though...

BIG IDEA #1 Show, Not Tell

Comics are brilliant at SHOWING (rather than TELLING) a story. We're going to have some fun, starting with this simple BORING image. Yawn.

It's not exactly thriling, darling!

Now we simply copy it. Exactly the same image.

BOOM! It's now a story. OK, a VERY BORING story... NOTHING HAPPENS. But perhaps that's part of the story.

Next, let's try changing something small in that second image...

Now we have a clue as to how fast time is passing. A minute? Ten? Twenty? The second image also gives us a clue to how our character might be FEELING. Is she late? Anxious? Why? Where is she going?

We've probably all been in a similar situation. We're drawn into the story. Still just two images, though. Let's try making a bigger change!

Ha! It's almost FUNNY now! Here's the magic of comics... The panel size, or layout, hasn't changed, but because of what we CHOOSE to SHOW, the gap in between the panels now *stands for* hours, not minutes.

How far can we go with it?

Now she's been there for a hundred years! Perhaps this is a little silly, but still funny ... and certainly a story.

We only used TWO panels, with no text, and we made a story that spans a hundred years. How would you make this idea even funnier? Have a go below!

Uncle Brian does a very funny thing with a banana skin...

13

ACTIVITY #1

Humans are so HARDWIRED to look for stories that we'll find stories anywhere. This can be a thing to look out for... Are you accidentally telling a different story? Try this game and see what you come up with.

 1 Take a look at the pictures in the first and last boxes. Think about the story you might tell to get from the first one to the last.

 2 Work out what the midpoint might look like and how you get from the start to the middle and then to the end.

 3 Fill in the midpoint first.

Start here!

 4 Now link the three together. Add more boxes if you need to.

To make it even more random and surprising...

 5 Grab a newspaper or magazine, some cereal boxes or some junk mail. Cut out the pictures and mix them up. Then pick two. Using the five boxes below, do a rough sketch of the first picture in the first box, and draw the second picture in the last box.

 6 Then come up with a story that joins the two pictures together. It doesn't matter how bizarre the story is, just that somehow they link together. You might be surprised with what you come up with!

START

MID

END

It can help to make your midpoint disastrous – like something has really gone wrong.

Something always goes wrong for me!

ACTIVITY #2

Here's a really good way to work out how to show a story. It's called Three Panel Fun. Pick your three favourite stories from TV shows, books or video games. In fact, anything with a story. Use Panel Strip A for the first story, B for the second and C for the third.

 Now draw in the START, the MIDDLE and the END of each story into the panel strips below.

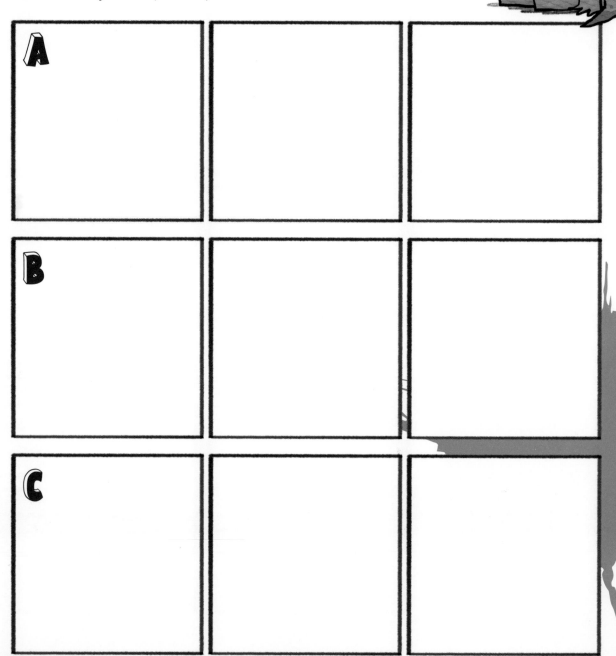

A

B

C

2 Could someone tell you what happens in the story by reading your comic? Where would you need to add extra panels? Pick your favourite story: A, B or C, bring over all three panels to the grid below, and use the extra panels to add in extra layers of storytelling. Make sure you put your first panel at the beginning and your last panel at the end. The panels in the middle are up to you!

START

MIDDLE?

MIDDLE?

MIDDLE?

END

Remember, you don't have to put your middle panel exactly in the middle. You can always move your story around.

A compelling story usually involves something or someone going through some kind of CHANGE, often in a surprising or satisfying way. Let's experiment!

 1 Start by drawing a thing, place or character in the first panel of your comic strip. Then in the last panel, draw the EXTREME opposite.

 2 Use the connecting panels to draw the event that happens in the middle. We've started you off with a couple of examples. Use the blank panels on the opposite page to create your own compelling stories!

 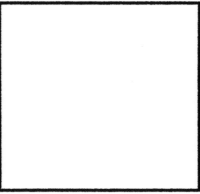 

 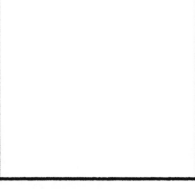 

Does this count as an opposite?

Upside down is definitely better than inside out!

What's the opposite of a banana?

BIG IDEA #2 What Happens in Your Story?

Before we get into any of the JUICY drawing, we need to have a good idea of what our story IS. What actually happens on the page?

We know that even the most simple of stories can be fluid and flexible. Stories change as we write them. So even if it's a simple idea, and even if you are CERTAIN you can see the WHOLE idea crystal clear in your head, it's still a good idea to get it all out ROUGHLY on paper, from beginning to end.

It lets you (and others) SEE your idea, as well as any bits that might be missing. It also frees up your brain to be really creative, as you don't have to hold everything in your head.

This process is called THUMBNAILING.

The idea is to draw lots of little 'thumbnail' drawings (they don't have to be THAT small! Sticky-note size is just right!), so you can work out what happens, if it makes sense and whether you can make it better.

Sticky notes are perfect for this, as you won't be tempted to do BEAUTIFUL ART, and they can be moved around, removed or added as the story develops.

If you don't have sticky notes, use a piece of A4 paper and cut it up into squares.

ACTIVITY #3

1 Now draw! Get it all down, as quickly as possible. Stick men, words, pictures, whatever is the quickest. Why not try to come up with a story to fit in the nine panels below?

Draw your own story, but if you're stuck, start with something BORING, or your least favourite chore...

They were called thumbnails because the drawings were literally the size of a thumbnail.

What SHAPE your idea is in at the start will vary from person to person, and from idea to idea.

You may have a FULL WRITTEN SCRIPT of your own, or from a friend, or you might be making a comic from your favourite book ... which is great as half the battle is won!

BUT USUALLY, a story starts with PART of an idea or SOME of the ingredients for the final thing.

You might have an idea for a character, or characters ... or maybe you have an idea about a particular place. You may want to deliver a particular message, joke or moral, or even just explore a particular mood or feeling. Jot and stick everything down, then you can start to put your ideas in order.

WHY ALL THIS PLANNING? I JUST WANT TO DRAW!

Go ahead! Some of the best comics are the simplest.

But a lot of making comics is about being CLEAR, and drawing the same things OVER AND OVER.

Having a rough plan will help you see how much work there is to do! You can make sure you fit everything that your story needs on to the page, and you won't do any unnecessary work.

I like plans.
Plans of sewers.

Every story is unique, but below you'll see some examples of why THUMBNAILING can be so useful. It shows up any holes in your story, or knowledge ... where you may need to add stuff or where you may need to take things away.

Even a simple comic takes considerable effort... Making a good plan can and will save you much heartache and struggle further down the line.

Think of the events of your story like locations on a map. There are three different ways to plan your journey or story...

1. ADVENTURE MODE! START AT THE BEGINNING AND GO!

You can set out without really knowing your end destination and go on a journey of discovery. You start at the beginning, draw and write and hope that you end up somewhere really cool.

This is great for generating and exploring ideas, characters, seeing the sights, being surprised! But it is possible to end up going round and round in circles, or getting lost.

GOOD IF YOU WANT TO EXPLORE CHARACTERS, IDEAS, A PLACE, A MOOD.

START

We're going in circles!

Where are we heading?

2. HUNTER MODE! MARK THE END, AND AIM AT IT!

This second way is more controlled ... you know where (how) you want your story to end, you mark it down on the map with an X and hunt it down. You'll see some sights along the way, but are always heading towards the final destination.

Maybe there's less opportunity for random discovery, but you will get to the end before you're exhausted or forget where you're going!

GOOD IF YOU WANT TO DELIVER A PUNCHLINE, A MESSAGE, A MORAL, A MYSTERY, A TWIST.

Hey, wait! What's this?

START

And this! Slow down.

Whoa! So direct, but maybe a little boring?

3. A BIT OF BOTH!

Again, it depends on the person and the story as to which technique is best. The truth is, a little of both techniques works well!

ADVENTURE MODE is great at first. Discover and flesh out your ideas and designs... THEN, when you've discovered where your story is going, switch into HUNTER MODE and plan the story, aiming at the ending, or punchline.

A good way to think of it is like telling a joke... The most important thing about a joke is that you deliver the punchline ... otherwise you're wasting everybody's time!

START

Ooh, I'm not sure where we're going...

... but we're progressing every step of the way

Another thing to think about before you choose your method of travel, is the effect you want your story to have. Is it funny? Should it scare people? Is it a fast-paced adventure? Or are you trying to create an emotion? These elements will have an impact on how you decide to plan your story and maybe stop you getting lost.

I never get lost. I have an unerring sense of direction...

In sewers, maybe...

Straight Lines and Circles

Drawing is just mark making. We can make LINES – straight lines, curved lines, clean lines or scraggly lines!

Here are some tips to help you draw straight lines quickly.

Put a dot where you want the line to start and another dot where you want the line to end.

Hovering above the paper, without putting the pencil on it, do some practice SWOOSHES between the dots.

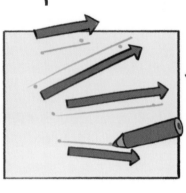

When you're ready, do three more swooshes! On the third one, put the pencil on the paper and draw the line. Did you hit both dots?

Draw lots of dots, and see how close you can get! Nobody can draw a perfect straight line (you're not a robot and that's GOOD!), but you will get good at straight lines pretty fast. Use some scrap paper to practise on.

When thumbnailing, you don't need to worry too much about being exact. Just work with the big shapes, quickly, to get your ideas down on paper. They are just for you to read, so they don't need to be beautiful.

My thumbnails are always beautiful!

Draw shorter lines from the wrist, longer lines from your elbow and ginormous lines from your shoulder.

Your lines will tend to be thicker at the end of the stroke than they are at the beginning.

I use my tail as a ruler – my straight lines are a little bumpy.

Now try circles...

Start swooshing in circles above the paper. When you're ready, put the pencil on the page and keep circling.

Drawing from your fingers or wrist will result in smaller circles. Drawing from your elbow, or even shoulder, will create bigger circles and longer curves. You might need a bigger piece of paper, to draw very large circles.

Turn the paper so your wrist is straight and comfortable for swooshing from your elbow!

BIG IDEA #3 Adding Words

So far we've focused on a comic's unique ability to tell stories purely with pictures ... but of course we can use text too!

Which part of your story you choose to SHOW (pictures) and which you choose to TELL (words) is up to you ... but it's generally a good idea to try and tell as much of your story as possible VISUALLY, and use text to link and support images ("Meanwhile..."), or speech, thoughts and sound effects.

See pages 82–94 for templates of speech bubbles, thought bubbles and how to draw amazing 3D lettering.

Speech bubbles

These show what a character is SAYING. You can even show that someone is whispering by using the dotted-line version of the speech bubble.

Thought bubbles

These show what a character is THINKING.

Caption box

This is similar to a narrator or voice-over. Often the words in a caption box set the scene or deal with time passing – one day later, for example.

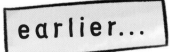

Sound effects

These are normally integrated into the artwork and show how the reader might hear the sound.

There are two big things to remember about using words in your comic that affects how you layout your artwork.

Firstly, words take up space. You need to leave enough space in your layouts for your speech bubbles or captions.

A panel that has text (and remember, not all panels need text) should probably split into two. Half for the art and half for the text. Remember, you don't HAVE to fill up half with text if you don't want to.

If a panel is becoming more than 50% words, then it's probably time to break the action in that panel into the next panel. You might need to have a rethink of your layout.

When thumbnailing, if you have a lot of text, sometimes it's helpful to write out your text on separate sticky notes at a decent readable size... Be honest! It's tempting to write TINY so you can scrape back some art space... But rather than ever-shrinking letters, try to find a way to trim the text down, or even better, find a way to show, not tell, and remove that text completely!

This way, you get no nasty suprises when you're laying out your proper page!

Secondly, text 'blocks' are read LEFT TO RIGHT, TOP TO BOTTOM.

This has an effect on the way you lay out your artwork... For instance, even in a simple set-up, with two characters having a conversation, it makes sense to place the character who speaks first on the left, so it feels natural, and flows in the right direction.

This can become a VERY STICKY problem the more complex your layout, or even when three characters are speaking... Again, the best thing to do is to have moveable thumbnail text, and be prepared to sacrifice the artwork layout for an easier read! Think of it as a FUN (but tricky) puzzle!

ACTIVITY #4

1 Use a pencil to draw the flow of the text on the comic below. Can you work out what you're supposed to read first?

So now it's time to add your words to your layout! Try to make the text add information the reader DIDN'T KNOW before, or AMPLIFY what's there already.

You can see a caption, a couple of speech bubbles, a thought bubble and a few sound effects.

The artwork has been nudged and overlapped so that everything feels integrated and has space to breathe.

ACTIVITY #5

1 Try adding speech bubbles, captions and sound effects to the comic strip below. Remember, not every picture needs words if you think it tells the story clearly enough on its own.

A font is the design of the type used for the letters and words in printed material or online. They have super-cool names and there are hundreds of thousands of different fonts in existence. Right now, we are using six different fonts in this books.

Main Heading
and Top Tip / Warm-up Title
Big Idea Title
BIG IDEA / TOP TIP

introductory text

main body text

speech bubble text

Auntie Audrey was a signwriter, she used to hang upside down to paint her words. Made it difficult for the rest of us to read them, though!

Before computers, letters were made from wooden or metal blocks and laid out by hand before printing.

We use different fonts to draw attention to different parts of the text on a page. You can stick to one font only and use it in different sizes and weights for emphasis. Here we've used the main body font for each sort of heading.

Main Heading

and Top Tip / Warm-up Title

Big Idea Title

BIG IDEA / TOP TIP

introductory text

body text

speech bubble text

Or you can choose to use multiple fonts as we have in this book.

Some illustrators or comic book artists like to hand letter. This means that they write out the text, often in a font they might have invented themselves.

Why don't you design your own font in the space below?

BIG IDEA #4 Characters and Props

Characters and props are the people and things that play a role in your story. It can be useful, and lots of fun, to explore and define what they look like before you start drawing them in your story.

You'll have to draw your characters and props over and over, so it's good to make yourself a 'model sheet'. This is a page which you look at to make sure that your design is the same throughout your story. This helps to keep who is who and what is what clear for the reader.

You can also take the time to simplify your design as much as possible to make your life easier.

This is called a 'character turnaround'. It's where you show your character from the front, the back and from the side.

It's also helpful to explore your character's facial expressions. How do they look when they're happy? How about sad or angry?

With your props, it's really fun and useful to explore how they might be used. How do the rocket boots work? What happens when you press that button on the watch?

Check out the next few pages to give you the basics on how to draw people and faces.

I'm not sure anything about this is easy...

Drawing People

Drawing people can seem tricky, but if you simplify body parts into SAUSAGE, EGG, CHIPS and BEANS, you'll soon discover an easy way to create poses.

First, take a coloured pencil and draw a sausage, an egg, two beans and two chips.

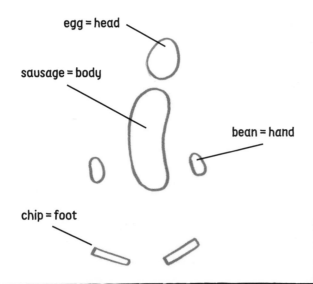

egg = head

sausage = body

bean = hand

chip = foot

Then join the shapes together with some spaghetti.

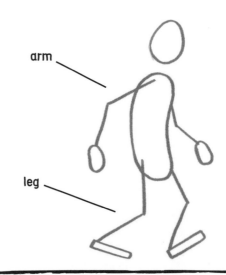

arm

leg

See how easy it is to create movement with some simple lines. Remember that the sausage can bend!

Now add details with a dark-coloured pencil.

ACTIVITY #6

 Use this page to draw lots of people moving in different ways. Are they sitting, running or doing a cartwheel. Place the sausage, egg, chips and beans and then join them up and add detail.

Add other objects

Overlap things

Play with size and shape

Try drawing me!

Or me?

Drawing Faces

Let's learn how to draw EXPRESSIVE faces – how to show someone looking happy, sad, angry or even VILLAINOUS simply using the eyes and the mouth.

Start by simplifying the eye down to LASH LINES and EYE BLOB.

The main thing you 'read' is the shape made by the lash lines that cover the pupil or eye blob.

Now you can add eyebrows and creases to amplify character and expression!

This works with lots of different styles. Try a few and have fun finding your own eye style!

I've got dots for eyes, but a very expressive nose cone.

Where eyes LOOK can add even more expression.

Closed eyes can still send a message.

Both eyes don't have to match, either!

ACTIVITY #7

Use the figures below to practise your eye expressions. What expression do you think goes with the pose? Is there more than one answer?

Big eyes are supposed to make you look cute!

Just like the eyes, humans are brilliant at reading mouth shapes for communication, but it can sometimes be difficult to capture the right expression when drawing. Don't worry, here are some tips to simplify things.

Simplify the mouth to where the lips meet the teeth (lip lines), teeth and a hole.

Look at the shapes made by contrasting areas. Top teeth against the dark inside of the mouth, or bottom teeth.

The mouth muscles and jaw create folds and dimples in the whole face as they move. These amplify the expression.

Experiment with different styles, but how you read expression will stay the same.

My favourite expression is SCARY!

Asymmetry is good. Both sides of the face don't need to look the same.

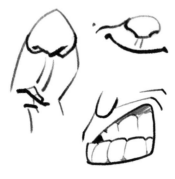

The mouth is three-dimensional. The lips wrap around the teeth and stretch up and back.

Gums, lips and moustaches all add character, but the rules stay the same.

ACTIVITY #8

 Draw your own mouth expression on the heads below. How does it change with the mouth open or closed?

It can help to look in a mirror to see how your mouth moves!

ACTIVITY #9

Right, let's take what we've learned and see if we can now draw some awesomely amazing heroes and some dastardly villains over the forms below.

 Think about your character's relative size to other characters, but also their proportions. How many 'heads high' are they?

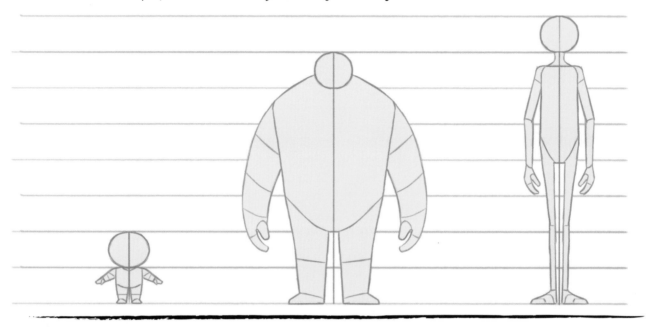

 Think in chunky shapes. This makes your character simpler to 'read', and simpler to draw. Think about the silhouette. Could you recognise your character in the dark?

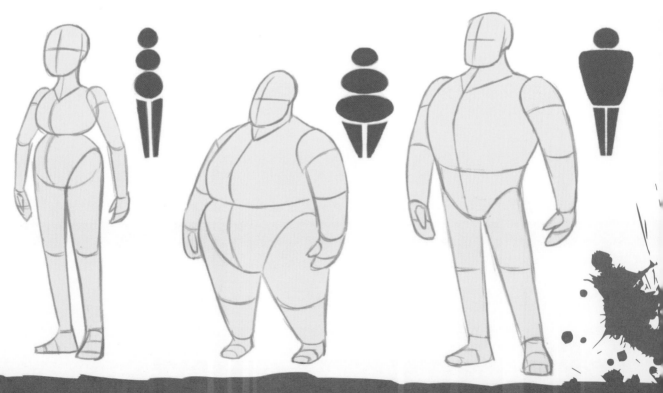

Heroes and villains can look like ANYTHING... It's often good to surprise the reader. A villainous fluffy teddy bear? A kindly fire-breathing dragon?

3 What would you add to these forms to make them look like heroes or villains? Have a go!

I think I would make a magnificent villain, darling!

Script Fun

Sometimes you might have the words of your dialogue already written. This is called a 'script'. Why not try drawing this simple script? Which part do you think will be the most complicated? Maybe start there and work backwards.

Use a pencil on these pages or sticky notes to plan your layout, and don't be afraid to try different approaches.

DOG - Hi, Cat.

CAT - Hi, Dog.

MOUSE ENTERS.

MOUSE - Hi, Cat. Hi, Dog.

DOG - Hi, Mouse.

CAT - Hi, Mouse.

Don't worry if you don't get it right first time – this can be quite tricky.

BIG IDEA #5 Environments and Vehicles

Just like your characters and the props they use, the environments your characters interact in also need to be drawn by you. Again, it's helpful and fun to explore them before you start drawing your story.

Think about your characters – where do they live? What sort of building is it?
Do they even live on Earth? The only limit is your imagination.

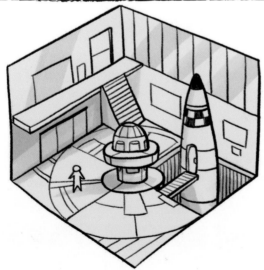

Do you need to know what a place looks like on the outside? Or on the inside? Or both? Take a look at your sketched-out story and make a list of the things your reader needs to know and what they don't need to know. That way you can save yourself a lot of time and effort if a particular setting doesn't get shown.

Vehicles can be both an environment – inside a plane cockpit or car – and a prop – something that's used by your characters. Think about whether you need to explore how something works before putting it in your story.

Planning your environments and vehicles is really good fun, so get creative. The process may inspire new ideas that enrich your story further ... or even inspire brand-new stories!

Check out the next few pages for some basic tips on perspective and overlap to give you a starting point on how to draw your environments and vehicles

I can ride a unicycle while peeling a banana!

Perspective and Overlap

Things look SMALLER the further away they are from you. This is called PERSPECTIVE. To draw things in the distance, it's helpful to think about something called the VANISHING POINT on the horizon.

Good examples are these desert telephone poles, or these wind turbines on the ocean.

See how they appear to move further away at regular intervals, while getting smaller and smaller towards the blue X. This is the VANISHING POINT – an imaginary point where the things you are looking at seem to disappear.

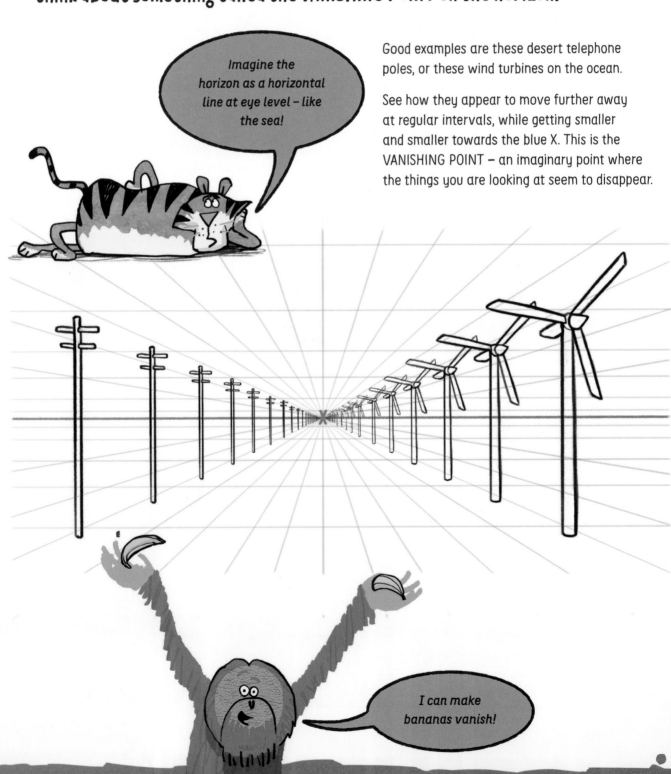

ACTIVITY #10

 Draw some rectangles on the grid below like the ones already there. Join the three corners of each rectangle that are closest to the vanishing point to that point.

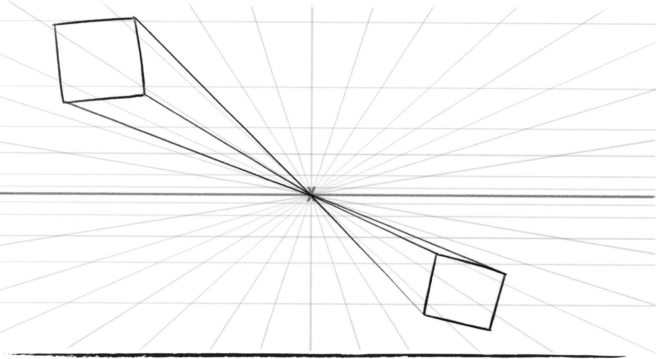

 Chop the boxes to the length you need. Now you have your boxes in perspective, you can fill them with whatever you want.

Practise first with box-like objects. Curvy, rounded things can be tricky! Breaking them into boxy chunks makes them easier to 'see' in perspective.

The vanishing point isn't always on the horizon (there might not be a 'horizon' in our picture if we are indoors, or in a forest, or looking up at a building, or down into a ravine). In these cases it might be better to call it an EYELINE. Sometimes you need to IMAGINE where that eyeline is when you are drawing.

If you want something to appear ABOVE the viewer, draw it above the EYELINE.

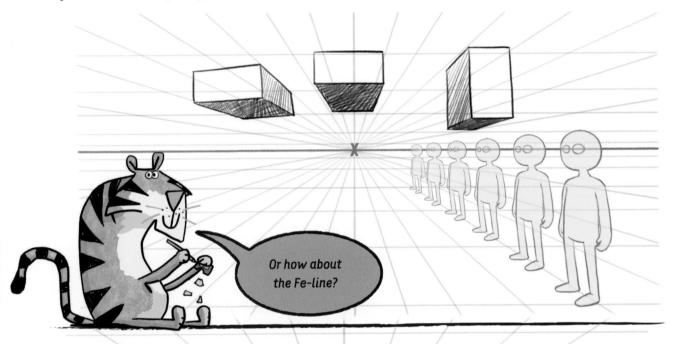

If you want something to appear BELOW the viewer, draw it below the EYELINE.

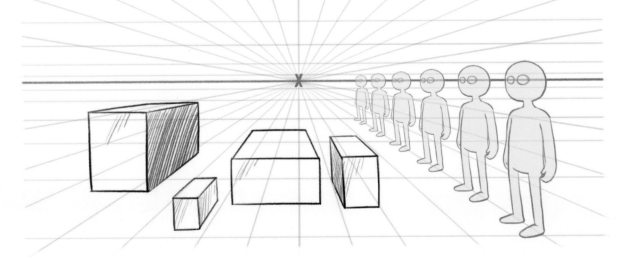

It can help to block in THE EXTREMES first. Think about not only what's right in front of you in the scene, but also what's highest? What's lowest? Once you've blocked those in, you can put in the mid-high and mid-low stuff ... then everything in between.

Even if you want to keep things flat and simple, the rules of perspective and overlap still apply. Cartoons often use this approach.

Keeping things simple sounds very sensible to me!

By choosing to ONLY use your overlap technique, you can still create a sense of depth.

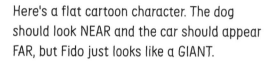

Here's a flat cartoon character. The dog should look NEAR and the car should appear FAR, but Fido just looks like a GIANT.

First, we need to move Fido off the horizon line. This simple change helps to 'sell' the depth of the flat shapes.

Then add a tree that overlaps the car, but is overlapped by the dog. Adding a path to connect them helps.

Then add in your detail. What else can you add to this picture to help 'sell' the depth? A house, the sun, some clouds?

Drawing Vehicles

If you can learn to draw a car, you can pretty much adapt that into any vehicle you wish. Just add wings, or a rotor. Take away two wheels and you have a motorbike.

A car is basically two boxes. One for sitting in and one for holding the engine. The wheels go somewhere BALANCED.

Let's draw it from the front and the side. Use simple shapes to create the details.

Apply what you learned about perspective to transfer that shape to a 3D box.

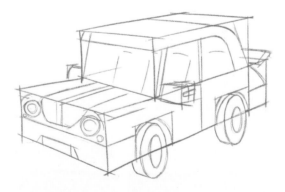

Sketch with your light-coloured pencil, shaving off and adding bits to the overall shape until you're happy. Finish with your dark-coloured pencil.

Remember to always add GO FASTER stripes.

54

ACTIVITY #11

1 Use this space to draw your own car. You can play with the design as you might play with a character. Add spoilers, exhaust pipes, cracks or scratches. Think about who might own it. Draw some whizzy lines underneath to make it look as if it's moving, or even FLYING off the ground.

I would love an ORANGUTANK!

TOP TIP #4 Foreshortening

We've been using our IMAGINARY X-RAY VISION to imagine horizons and vanishing points that we can't see to draw with PERSPECTIVE. It's time to use the things we can see. Another great technique to make sure our pictures have DEPTH is to use the way objects OVERLAP each other.

These houses go back into the distance...

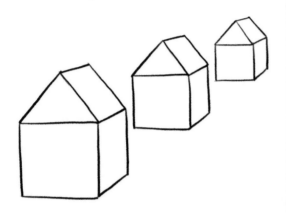

But THESE houses REALLY look as if they are one in front of the other.

Use your light-coloured pencil to sketch in a box for each house, and then with your dark pencil, draw only the parts that would show!

It's not just separate objects that overlap each other. WHOLE THINGS OVERLAP THEMSELVES. This is called FORESHORTENING (a posh way of saying PERSPECTIVE and OVERLAP). See how the separate 'lumps' of the cat combine and overlap!

Seems a little harsh!

ACTIVITY #12

1 Here's a vanishing point and some guidelines. Complete the scene below remembering to use your overlap and foreshortening skills! Think about which character overlaps the other as it can really change where they exist in the scene.

Here's how
I overlap!

BIG IDEA #6 Do Your Layout

Wow, that's a LOT of planning ... but hopefully it's been fun, and you've got a really good idea of what you're going to make. Now it's time to start an actual page!

So we have our thumbnailed comic. The words and pictures that tell our story.

But they're all on sticky notes / in squares the same size. This works brilliantly for some kinds of comics – usually humourous stories and short gags work great as a clear, simple, direct layout.

But what if we want to do something a little more dynamic, if our story has a bit more variation to its rhythm and more action? We want to engage the reader.

You can think about the visual rhythm of your story panels like a piece of music – quiet to loud, down tempo to up tempo, building and crashing through crescendos. This keeps it interesting.

Or think about a roller coaster, the slow parts BUILD TENSION for the faster parts. There's a balance of texture.

We're going to continue with the bus stop story used earlier... We've got all the words and the pictures, in fact we have the whole page, but the panels are boring and square.

So how can we lay this out on the page so it's engaging and clear?

By changing the panel sizes, we can adjust the rhythm and pace of the story. We can make the first panel wide to set the scene. The second panel can shrink to allow the first panel to widen. Doing this also allows us to focus on the character's actions.

Next, we make our big, surprising moment extra large – it's up to you how many panels to use.

The facial reaction shot is now an inset. It doesn't obscure the BIG moment, but implies that the reaction is happening at the same time.

If you're really clever, you can plan the big suprises to happen on the page turn! Assuming your comic has pages!

I like the idea of focusing on my face, darling!

ACTIVITY #13

 Take the storyline you created on page 21 and create a layout to match. You decide where to emphasise the action with more space. Simply draw your frame over the dotted guideline. You might not fit all the story into this page, but don't worry, this is just to practise the process. Or, if you prefer, use the cat and dog storyline below.

If you have sticky notes, you could use them here!

To make your comic as dramatic and dynamic as possible, it's great to show lots of action on the page. Here are some tips to help you add impact to your drawings.

Use lots of straight lines! Hard edges with lots of contrast imply speed.

Hard or acute angles also do a similar thing. When your image is horizontal, things feel safe and calm. If they move off the horizontal, you feel unsettled.

Another way to increase the tension and action in a scene is to build up to the final moment using multiple panels.

 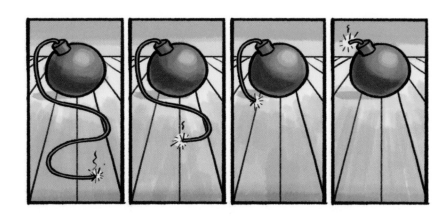

ACTIVITY #14

1 Fill in the panels below to illustrate this rocket taking off. What would you show?

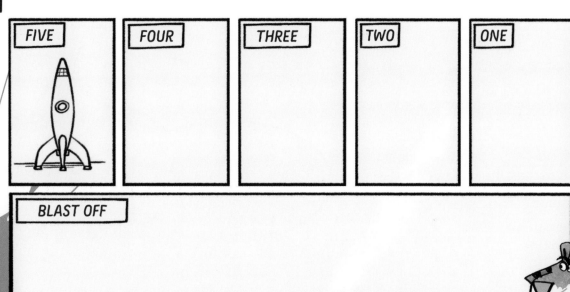

FIVE   FOUR   THREE   TWO   ONE

BLAST OFF

I could take off like a rocket... If I wanted to, that is...

HOORAY! Your comic is probably already looking great, but most comics will be taken at least one more step past the sketch stage. Not only to make them look nice, but for clarity for the reader too.

If you LOVE your comic as it is, don't feel you HAVE to take it any further! A handmade feel can be one of the best things about comics. It shows that a human ... or Orangutan ... made it!

Ahem... What are you saying, exactly?

Remember, the final 'look' or style of your comic is entirely up to you. Your options are as broad as your imagination ... watercolour, photography, written in strawberry jam?

But the majority of comics tend to be created with drawings or 'linework'. For some that's all they need! Others are given a layer of tone, or colour, to punch them up further.

I love strawberry jam, it's definitely my favourite flavour!

Let's start with linework.

Did you know that most comic book artists work at TWICE THE SIZE as the final printed comic? This makes it much easier on the hands and eyes when doing detail! So don't feel discouraged if copying a printed comic feels IMPOSSIBLE ... the original might be a lot bigger!

To keep linework nice and clean, it's best to work on a new sheet of paper laid over your pencil roughs.

If you like, captions and bubbles can be made seperately, if it makes your linework easier.

Clip your sheets together to keep them in the same place and the drawings aligned.

Use a ruler to draw the panels. Or you could go freehand for a looser look.

Are you going to use a pen, a pencil or an inky brush? The choice is yours, but choose a medium you feel comfortable and confident using.

Waterproof ink is also a good idea, especially if you're going to add colour later.

Use a lightbox, or a window, to make it easier to see the roughs through the new sheet of paper.

A common comic book artist trick is to do all your pencil roughs in NON-PHOTO-BLUE PENCIL! This blue is INVISIBLE to photocopiers, and easily removed digitally. This means you can work DIRECTLY on to the same page, safe in the knowledge that the blue pencil will not be seen.

Again, here we can see how text/inset artwork can be made separately, and put together at the end.

Most comics you can buy will have been put together digitally. All this means is that everything is on digital layers in a file, rather than layers of paper and glue!

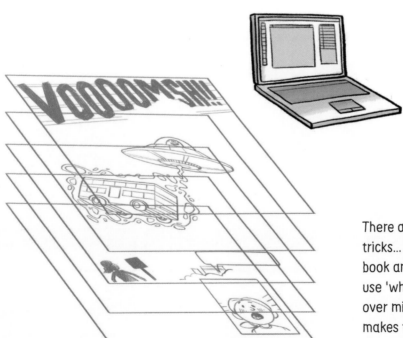

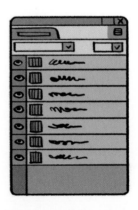

There are no rules! Just tricks... The best comic book artists in the world use 'whiteout' or stick bits over mistakes. Whatever makes the comic work!

A quick note on tangents...

I thought they were men who liked sunbeds!

Aren't they a bit like satsumas?

No! A tangent is where two lines meet, but do not overlap.

Our drawings are FULL of meeting lines, of course ... but in the wrong place, it can make your drawing confusing. This usually happens when a foreground thing LOOKS as if it shares a line with a background object.

Here are some examples of tangents. You'll usually avoid tangents instinctively as you draw, but if anything ever looks 'off'... look for unwanted tangents.

This is better. A good rule is to 'OVERLAP or FRAME'. Either you fully tuck one thing behind another, or you fully give each shape its own space. Keep it clear and simple.

Why not practise your linework here before working on your own roughs!

Here are some sketches in pencil. Try using each of the items listed below to produce the final artwork for the scene.:

· hard pencil   · soft pencil   · fibretip pen   · ballpoint pen   · brush with ink

Remember, you can always work larger than this page if it lets you use the medium you love.

This one is slightly more tricky.

Here's a pencilled scene with lots ot potential tangents. Using your linework skills over the top, clean up the drawing to remove as many of the tangents as you can.

I think it would be nicer if it were banana cake!

BIG IDEA #8 Using Tone

Now you have completed your linework, you may want to add tone to your comic. This can add drama and capture your reader's imagination. Let's have a quick look at how to add light and shade to your linework.

THE VISIBLE WORLD IS JUST LIGHT AND SHADE. Artists use TONE to replicate how light and shadow falls across 3D objects. You can choose a TONAL RANGE for your drawing, or it might be steered by the tonal range of the pen or pencil you are using.

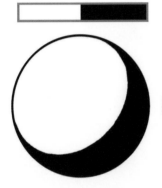

This range uses ONLY BLACK and WHITE.

This range uses BLACK, WHITE and a MIDTONE.

This one has two more distinct tones. Let's call them MID-MIDTONES.

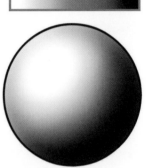

This last one uses the whole range!

ACTIVITY #15

 Using your dark-coloured pencil, can you fill in the boxes below to reproduce the shading you see on the spheres above?

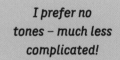

I prefer no tones – much less complicated!

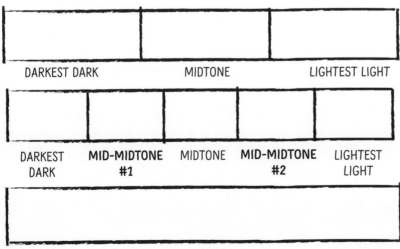

| DARKEST DARK | MIDTONE | LIGHTEST LIGHT |

| DARKEST DARK | MID-MIDTONE #1 | MIDTONE | MID-MIDTONE #2 | LIGHTEST LIGHT |

| DARKEST DARK | MIDTONE | LIGHTEST LIGHT |

2 Now you've mastered the different tones, see if you can apply them to the spheres below. Think about where the light strikes each of them. Use only three tones for this exercise.

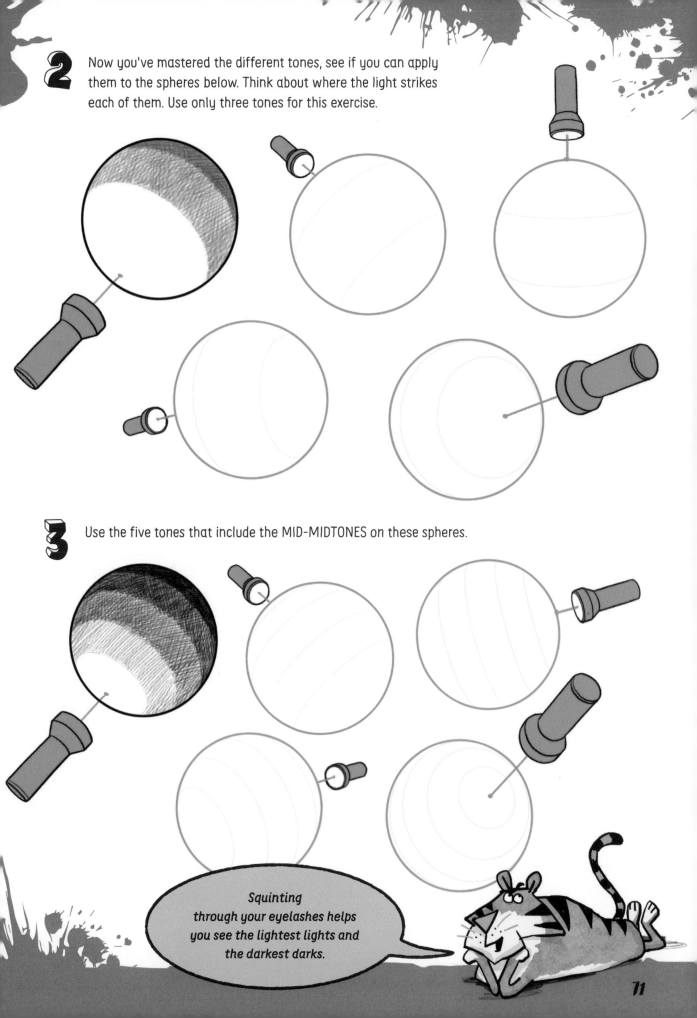

3 Use the five tones that include the MID-MIDTONES on these spheres.

Squinting through your eyelashes helps you see the lightest lights and the darkest darks.

ACTIVITY #16

1 Now it's time to try applying your skills to objects. Use the five tones that include the MID-MIDTONES to complete the picture below. Where does the light and shadow fall?

ACTIVITY #17

This activity uses the whole range of tones! Even though we're not separating them into DISTINCT tones, you start the same way.

 See if you can complete this scene using everything you have learned about light, shade and tone.

I think I would like to be the first crocodile in space!

Let's Add Tone

There are as many ways to make comic art as there are to make pictures... Do it your way! You will need to consider whether to complete your comic in black and white or colour. Remember that adding tone and colour CONSIDERABLY multiplies the amount of work it will take to finish!

Don't feel as if black and white is any 'less' than full colour. Black and white can look punchy and powerful, and bold. Use line and midtones with hatching or ink wash.

Using a limited palette looks striking and can work well with a contrast colour as a ZINGER!

Full-colour artwork can still be done relatively quickly if you use blocks of flat colour.

This is very time consuming. Full-colour artwork with every detail captured – each panel a work of art in itself. Good luck!

ACTIVITY #18

1 Let's explore a limited palette – or small range of colours. Choose one colour that you want to use as your main colour. Fill in the circles below using that colour.

2 Next, pick a totally DIFFERENT colour, a real contrast... This is your ZINGER. Fill in the ZINGER circle.

3 Now use your two colours to fill in this lineworked comic. Where will you choose to put your ZINGER colour?

Sniff... Oh, SO SAD... Sniff ... but the dinosaurs were OK in the end, right?

Let me make you a cup of tea, and we'll have a chat.

Wet Versus Dry

If you're using dry media, such as pencils or pens, to colour your comic, then jump right in... Just as you would in a colouring book. However, if you want to use wet media, such as ink washes or watercolour paints, then you need to be sure you keep your lovely linework from running, bleeding and making everything muddy.

Here are a couple of approaches you could use if you want to use wet colour.

Use waterproof pens, pencils or inks to draw your linework first, THEN go in with your colour.

OR add your colour FIRST. Then, once your page is dry, you can add your linework over the top.

The comics you can buy will have been separated into these layers digitally, so they can be printed cleanly.

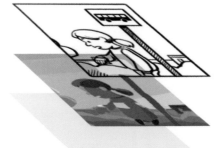

A fun thing to try is to put your A4 pencil roughs into a plastic pocket. Do your linework in permanent marker on the outside. Slide out your pencils, and colour. Slide it back in and instantly you have CLEAN layers!

You can then scan or photocopy this to make MULTIPLES!

ACTIVITY #19

It can be helpful to work out what the TONAL value
will be before jumping straight into colour.

 Use only black and white to colour in the first panels below. Don't forget
to use your hatching techniques to show light and shade.

It's heart-rending!
Don't worry, cousin, we'll
remember you!

Now move on to full colour here. Use the tonal page to help you keep your brights bright and your darks dark.

Right, it's time to put all your skills to the test and create your very own comic. Why not use the story you've worked on in the earlier activities to start you off? Or if you have another brilliant story just bursting to leap on to the page, simply work through each BIG IDEA using your brand-new idea.

Check out the templates at the back of the book – they might speed things up for you!

When drawing comics, it's a good idea to make a dummy book to plan your story in! This way, you can easily see at what point you reach a page turn. It's also useful to have a limited amount of pages to make sure your story ENDS and is exciting.

Also, you will have an ACTUAL BOOK in your hands which you can give to your friends. Want a bigger comic? Use a sheet of A3 paper instead.

Take a piece of A4 paper. Fold it in half three times so that the page is split into eight equal rectangles.

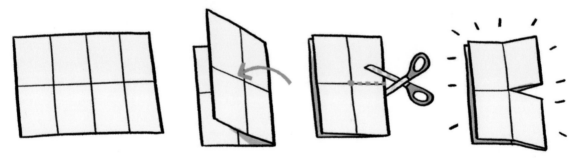

Fold in half. Using a pair of scissors, snip across the fold, halfway to the centre, then unfold.

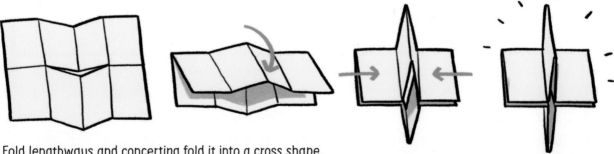

Fold lengthways and concertina fold it into a cross shape.

Write page numbers and arrows to show the 'right way up'. This means when you unfold it, you can make sure you're drawing your pages the right way up!

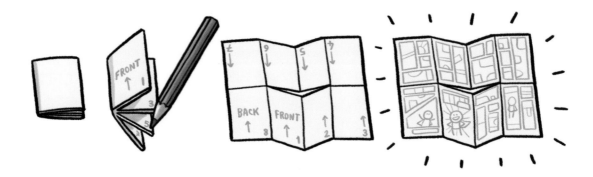

To make copies, unfold your comic. Copy it flat, then fold each copy the same way, snip to the middle and refold. You can now give (or sell!) your comic to friends and family.

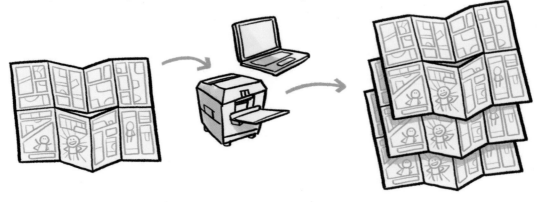

Use both sides! Perhaps you could draw a poster of your favourite character!

I'm not sure I'm going to be able to manage the paper folding!

I bet Tiger thinks he should be on both sides of the poster!

So Can You Draw Comics?

Well done for getting this far.

You have learned how to plan your story and layout your art.

You've created characters and settings. You've included action and humour, and you know how to add tension and drama to your story.

Why not write about MEEE? Mine is a fascinating tail...

You've added words to your tale! You've used speech bubbles, captions and sound effects.

ROAARRRR! AARGGGGH! Just practising my sound effects.

You've learned how to ink and add tone and colour.

Gosh, I think I've got it!

You've practised your linework and can make a dummy comic. You know all about fonts, and how to use foreshortening and perspective. You understand what makes a comic!

Wow, we're all really good at drawing comics. What shall we draw next?

Congratulations! You can draw comics!

Speech Bubbles

Here are some different types of speech bubbles you could use.
Simply trace over the shape and apply it to your panel.

Thought Bubbles

Here are some thought bubbles you could use. Simply trace over the shape and add it to your comic strip.

Sound Effects

Here are some example sound effects for you to copy. Either trace over the shape or redraw in place.

KAPOW!

ZAP!

BOOM!

SPLAT!

ZOOOOM!

POW!

3D Lettering

Remember, you can also make lettering or symbols or even titles 3D, so they really stand out. Follow the same perspective rules you learned earlier (see page 50) to really punch up your graphic design.

Perspective Grids

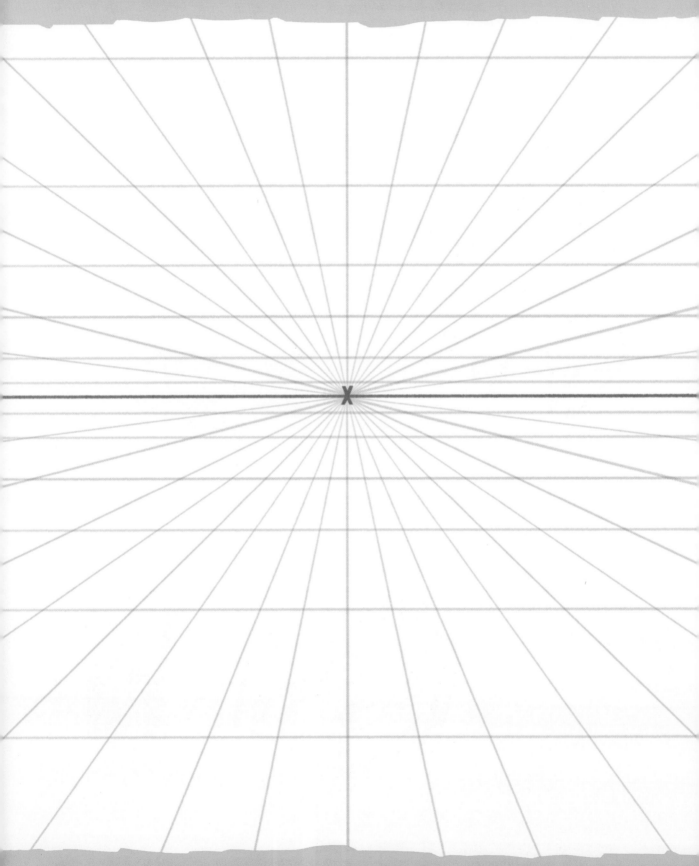

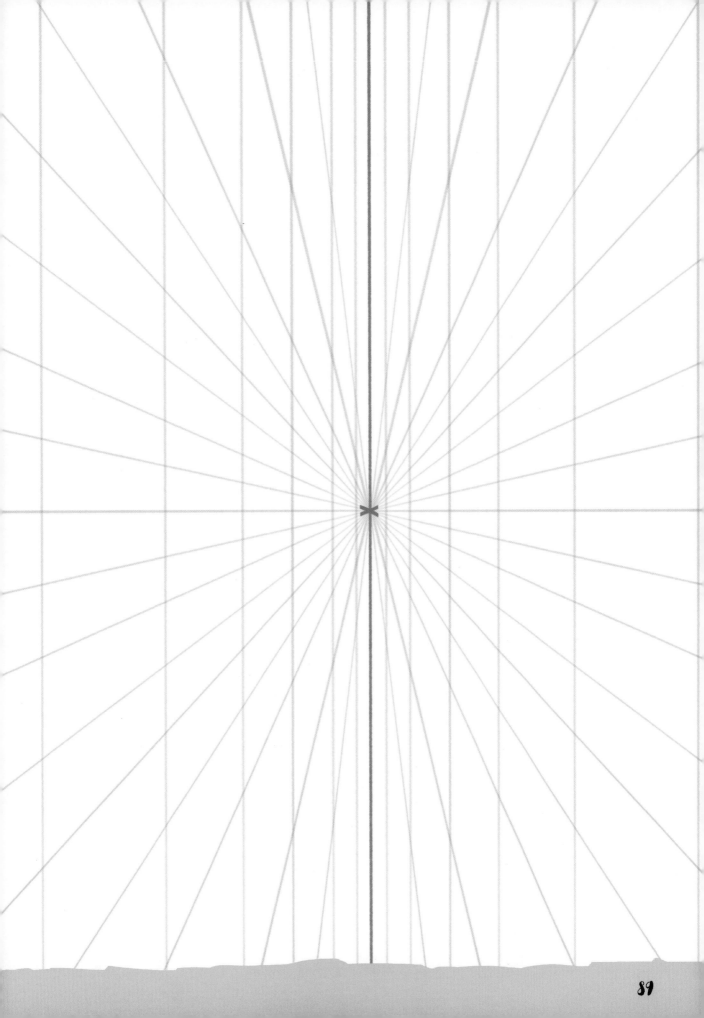

Draw Your Own Panel Frames

Trace through on to another sheet using the grid on the right when planning out a page. Of course, you can lay out your comic according to what you need, but this will help you get sketching quickly. Below are examples of how you can split up a page of panels.

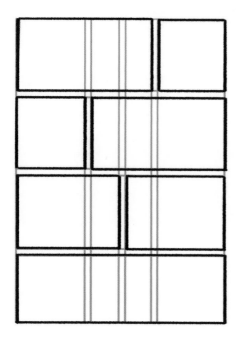

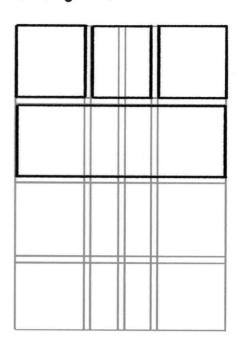

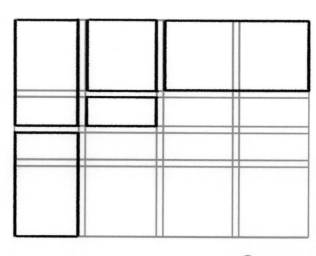

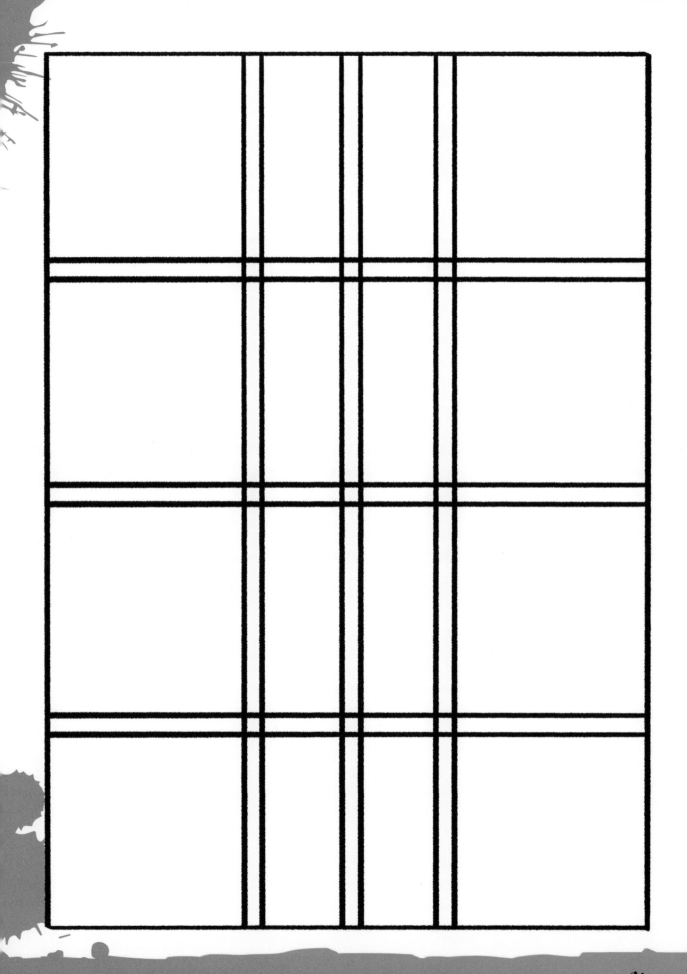

Practice Panel Frames

The next three pages have lots of different panel frame combinations you can choose to use for your comic.

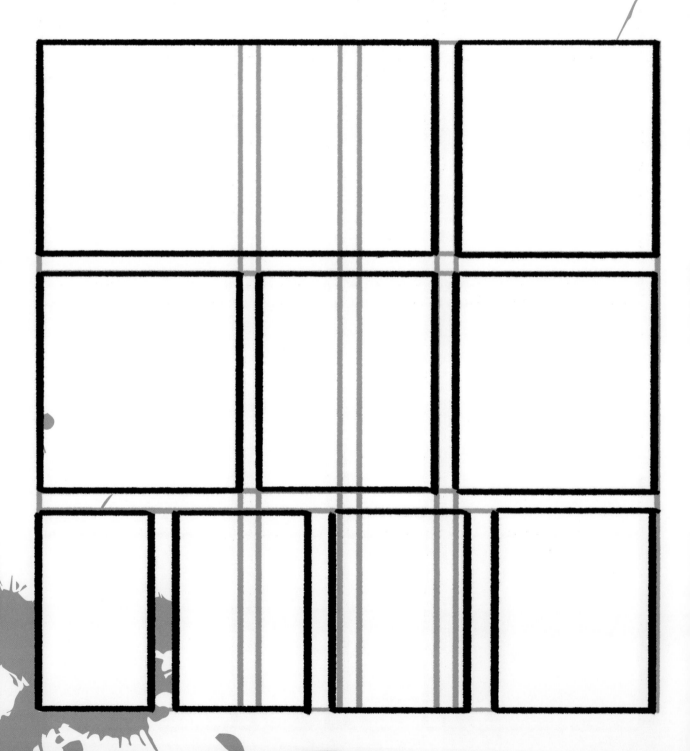

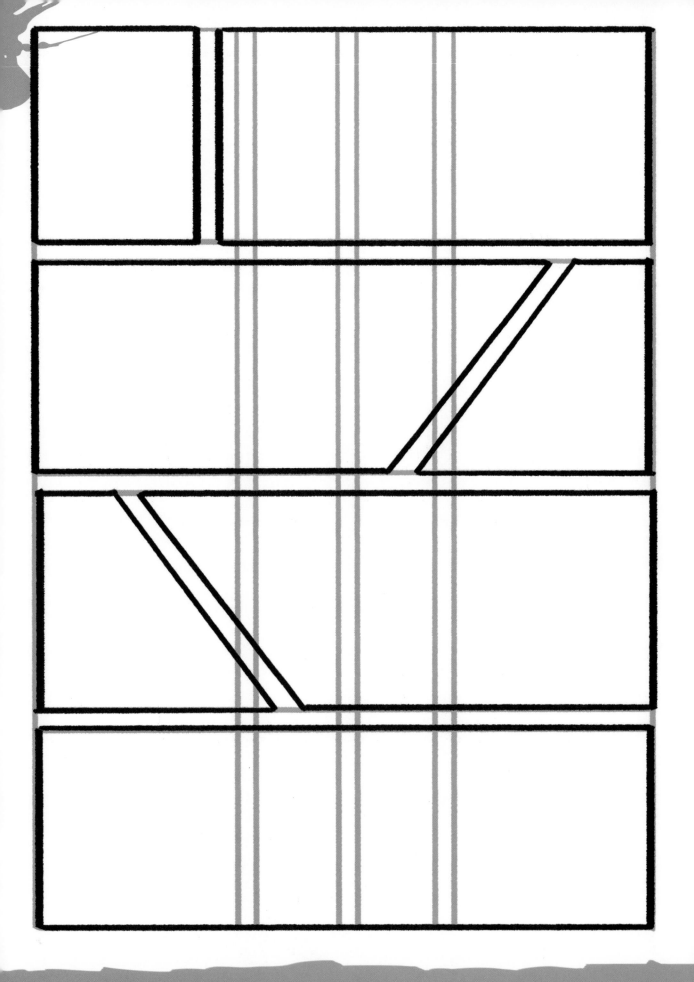

Index